WITH A CD OF PIANO
ACCOMPANIMENTS

LOW VOICE

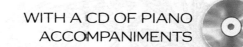

15 ART SONGS BY AMERICAN COMPOSERS

SONGS BY
ARGENTO, BERNSTEIN, CHANLER, COPLAND, DUKE, HUNDLEY, AND ROREM

BOOSEY & HAWKES

AN IMAGEM COMPANY

DISTRIBUTED BY

HAL•LEONARD®
CORPORATION
7777 W. BLUEMOUND RD. P.O. BOX 13819 MILWAUKEE, WI 53213

For all works contained herein:
Unauthorized copying, arranging, adapting, recording, Internet posting, public performance, or other distribution of the
printed or recorded music in this publication is an infringement of copyright.
Infringers are liable under the law.

www.boosey.com
www.halleonard.com

CONTENTS

Pianist on the CD: Laura Ward

for Nicholas Di Virgilio

Winter

from *Six Elizabethan Songs*
original key: a major 3rd higher

WILLIAM SHAKESPEARE

DOMINICK ARGENTO

In accompaniment recording, the first vocal note is played three times before the entrance.

© Copyright 1970 by Boosey & Hawkes, Inc. Copyright Renewed.
New transposition © Copyright 2006 by Boosey & Hawkes, Inc.
Copyright for all countries. All rights reserved.

sings   the   star - ing   owl

Tu - whoo!   Tu - whit!   Tu - whoo!

A mer - ry   note!

While greas - y Joan doth keel the

pot

When all a - loud the wind doth blow, _____

And cough-ing drowns the par - son's saw, _____ And birds sit brood-ing in the

8

for Nicholas Di Virgilio

Spring

from *Six Elizabethan Songs*

original key: a minor 3rd higher

THOMAS NASH

DOMINICK ARGENTO

© Copyright 1970 by Boosey & Hawkes, Inc. Copyright Renewed.
New transposition © 2006 by Boosey & Hawkes, Inc.
Copyright for all countries. All rights reserved.

Spring is like a perhaps hand

from *Songs about Spring*

original key: a minor 3rd higher

e.e. cummings

DOMINICK ARGENTO

© Copyright 1980 by Boosey & Hawkes, Inc. Copyright Renewed.
New transposition © 2006 by Boosey & Hawkes, Inc.
Text: © Copyright 1923, 1925, 1949, 1951 by e.e. cummings
Reprinted by permission of Harcourt, Brace & Jovanovich, Inc.
Copyright for all countries. All rights reserved.

Jupiter has seven moons

from *I Hate Music!*

original key: a minor 3rd higher

Words and Music by
LEONARD BERNSTEIN

© Copyright 1943 by M. Witmark & Sons. Copyright Renewed by Warner Bros. Inc.
Leonard Bernstein Music Publishing Company LLC, Publisher.
Boosey & Hawkes, Inc., Sole Agent.
New transposition © 2006 by Boosey & Hawkes, Inc.

The man in the moon would be gi - gan - tic!

But we have on - ly one!

On - ly

one!

I hate music!

from *I Hate Music!*

original key: a minor 3rd higher

Words and Music by
LEONARD BERNSTEIN

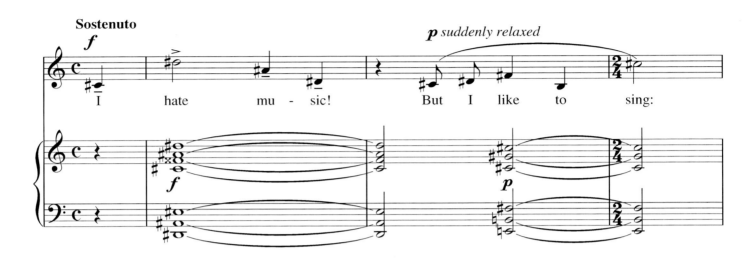

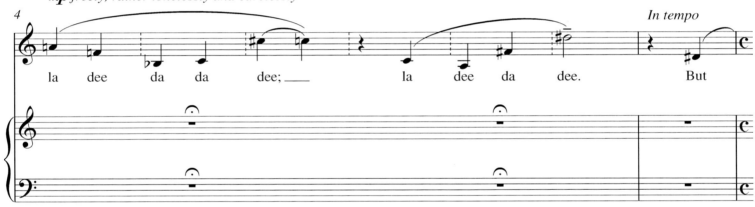

In accompaniment recording, the first vocal note is played three times before the entrance.

© Copyright 1943 by M. Witmark & Sons. Copyright Renewed by Warner Bros. Inc.
Leonard Bernstein Music Publishing Company LLC, Publisher.
Boosey & Hawkes, Inc., Sole Agent.
New transposition © 2006 by Boosey & Hawkes, Inc.

These, My Ophelia

original key: E♭ Major

ARCHIBALD MACLEISH

THEODORE CHANLER

Copyright 1936 by Cos Cob Press Inc., New York, Renewed 1962.
Copyright and renewal assigned to Boosey & Hawkes, Inc.
New transposition © 2006 by Boosey & Hawkes, Inc.
Copyright for all countries. All rights reserved.

Ching-a-ring Chaw

(Minstrel Song)

from *Old American Songs, Set II*

original key: D Major

Arranged by
AARON COPLAND

© Copyright 1954 by The Aaron Copland Fund for Music, Inc. Copyright Renewed.
New transposition © 2005 by The Aaron Copland Fund for Music, Inc.
Boosey & Hawkes, Inc., Sole Publisher & Licensee.
All rights reserved.

39

style,　Coach with　four white hor - ses,　There the eve - nin'

43

meal,　Has one two three four cour - ses._____

48 *mp*

8vb ♩

Ching-a-ring-a ring ching, ching - a ring ching, Ho - a ding-a ding kum lar - kee,

mp

52

Ching-a - ring - a ring ching, Ho - a ding kum lar - kee._____

56

f

Nights we all will dance,　To the harp and

f

sf

To Ingolf Dahl
Why do they shut me out of Heaven?
from *Twelve Poems of Emily Dickinson*
original key: a minor 3rd higher

EMILY DICKINSON

AARON COPLAND

Moderately (♩ = 76)

Why do they shut me out of Heav-en _____ Did I sing too loud?

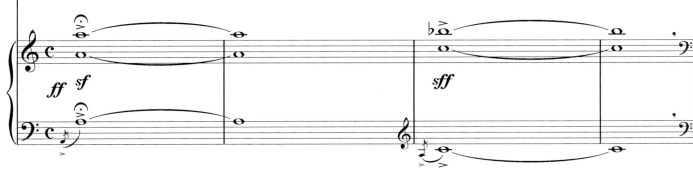

But I can sing a lit-tle min-or, _____ Tim-id as a bird.

Would-n't the an-gels try me just once more Just see if I

© Copyright 1951 by The Aaron Copland Fund for Music, Inc. Copyright Renewed.
Boosey & Hawkes, Inc., Sole Publisher & Licensee.
New transposition © 2006 by The Aaron Copland Fund for Music, Inc.
Copyright for all countries. All rights reserved.
Text from *Poems of Emily Dickinson*, edited by Martha Dickinson
and Alfred Leete Hampson, by permission of Little, Brown and Company.

To Marcelle de Manziarly

Heart, we will forget him

from *Twelve Poems of Emily Dickinson*

original key: E♭ Major

EMILY DICKINSON

AARON COPLAND

* Grace note on the beat

© Copyright 1951 by The Aaron Copland Fund for Music, Inc. Copyright Renewed.
Boosey & Hawkes, Inc., Sole Publisher & Licensee.
New transposition © 2006 by The Aaron Copland Fund for Music, Inc.
Copyright for all countries. All rights reserved.
Text from *Poems of Emily Dickinson*, edited by Martha Dickinson
and Alfred Leete Hampson, by permission of Little, Brown and Company.

To the memory of my grandmother

The Astronomers
(An Epitaph)
original key: a major 2nd higher

RICHARD HUNDLEY

Based on an inscription
found in Allegheny, Pa.

© Copyright 1961 by Boosey & Hawkes, Inc. Copyright Renewed.
Revised version © Copyright 1970 by Boosey & Hawkes, Inc.
New transposition © 2006 by Boosey & Hawkes, Inc.
Copyright for all countries. All rights reserved.

Sept. 1959, New York City

Jeanie with the Light Brown Hair

original key

STEPHEN FOSTER
arranged by
NED ROREM

© Copyright 1990 by Boosey & Hawkes, Inc.
Copyright for all countries. All rights reserved.

soft sum-mer air. _____ I

long for Jean-ie with the day - dawn_ smile, Ra - diant in glad - ness,

warm with win - ning guile; I hear her mel - o - dies, like

joys gone_ by Sigh-ing round my heart_ o'er the fond hopes that die:

Sigh-ing like the night wind and sob-bing like the rain,

Wail-ing for the lost one that comes not a-gain: I

long for Jean-ie and my heart bows _ low, Nev-er more to find her where the

bright wa-ters flow.

O Do Not Love Too Long

original key

WILLIAM BUTLER YEATS

NED ROREM

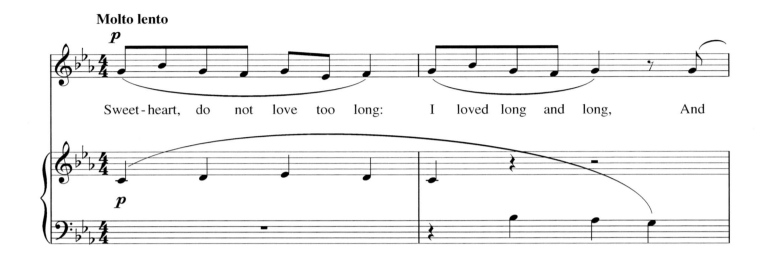

Sweet-heart, do not love too long: I loved long and long, And

grew to be out of fash - ion ____ Like an old ____ song. All

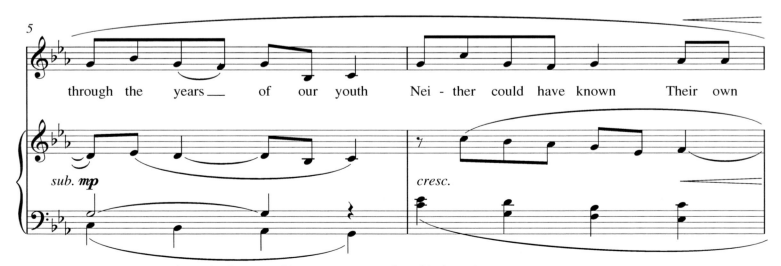

through the years ____ of our youth Nei - ther could have known Their own

In accompaniment recording, the first vocal/piano notes are played before the entrance.

© Copyright 1990 by Boosey & Hawkes, Inc.
Copyright for all countries. All rights reserved.

Marrakech, 20 April 1951

To Julien Green

What if some little pain...

original key: a minor 3rd higher

EDMUND SPENSER

NED ROREM

© Copyright 1952 by Hargail Music Press; Renewed 1980.
Copyright and Renewal assigned to Boosey & Hawkes, Inc.
New transposition © Copyright 2008 by Boosey & Hawkes, Inc.
Copyright for all countries. All rights reserved.

Fez, Morocco, 20 December 1949
(14:30)

Central Park at Dusk

original key: a major 3rd higher

SARA TEASDALE*

JOHN DUKE

*From "Collected Poems" by Sara Teasdale (Macmillan)

© Copyright 1949 by Boosey & Hawkes, Inc. Copyright renewed.
New transposition © 2006 by Boosey & Hawkes, Inc.
Copyright for all countries. All rights reserved.

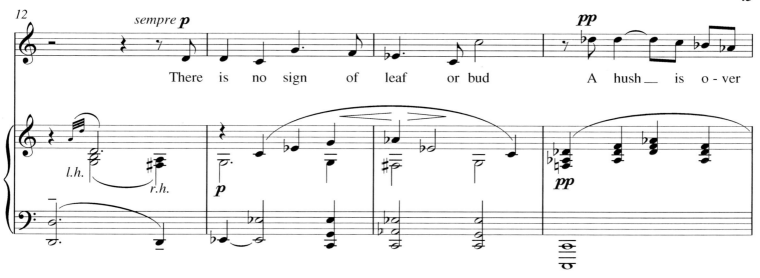

There is no sign of leaf or bud A hush is o-ver

eve-ry-thing. Si - lent as wom-en wait for love

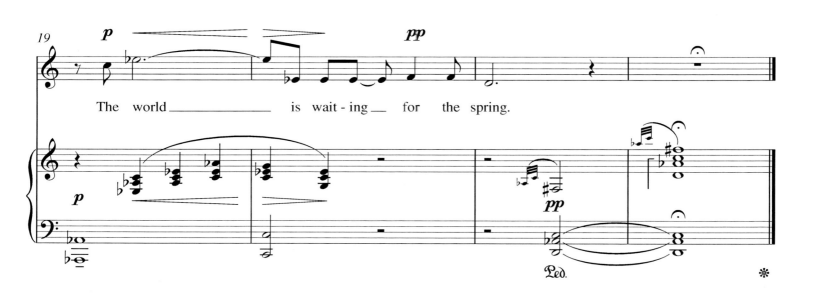

The world is wait-ing for the spring.

There will be stars

original key: A minor

SARA TEASDALE*

JOHN DUKE

There will be stars ___ o-ver the place for-ev-er;

Though the house we loved ___ and the street we loved ___

___ are lost, Ev-'ry time the

*From "Collected Poems" by Sara Teasdale (Macmillan)

© Copyright 1953 by Boosey & Hawkes, Inc. Copyright renewed.
New transposition © 2006 by Boosey & Hawkes, Inc.
Copyright for all countries. All rights reserved.